LEAVES OF GOLD

A Special Gift

For:

Denise Bell

From:

Miriam Loyo

Date:

December 1999

Happy Birthday !!!

Cherished Moments Gift Books

A Basket of Friends

Leaves of Gold™
An Inspirational Classic for Our Time

Merry Christmas With Love

Once Upon a Memory
Reflections of Childhood

Seeds of Kindness
Garden Thoughts for the Heart

Sweet Rose of Friendship

Tea for Two
Taking Time for Friends

Where Angels Dwell
A Treasury of Hope, Inspiration and Blessing

Leaves of Gold™

Brownlow

Brownlow Publishing Company, Inc.

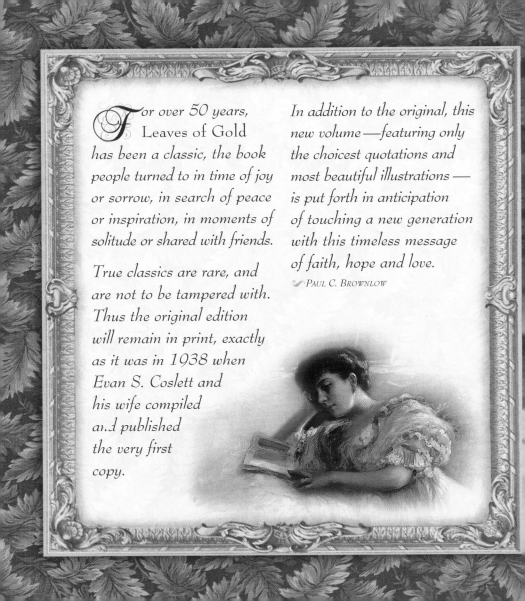

For over 50 years, Leaves of Gold has been a classic, the book people turned to in time of joy or sorrow, in search of peace or inspiration, in moments of solitude or shared with friends.

True classics are rare, and are not to be tampered with. Thus the original edition will remain in print, exactly as it was in 1938 when Evan S. Coslett and his wife compiled and published the very first copy.

In addition to the original, this new volume—featuring only the choicest quotations and most beautiful illustrations—is put forth in anticipation of touching a new generation with this timeless message of faith, hope and love.

PAUL C. BROWNLOW

LEAVES OF GOLD

Contents

Accomplishments.................. 8

Adversity............................ 11

Beauty............................... 14

Courage.............................. 18

Education............................ 20

Faith.................................. 23

Friendship.......................... 26

Gratitude............................ 30

Happiness........................... 33

Heartstrings........................ 36

Home & Family................ 38

Immortality........................ 42

Joy..................................... 46

Kindness............................ 50

Life Lessons...................... 54

Love.................................. 61

Nature's Garden................ 66

Possessions........................ 70

Prayer................................ 72

Serenity............................. 76

Serving Others.................. 80

Spiritual Insights.............. 84

Today................................ 88

Worthwhile Thoughts........ 92

Accomplishment

I find the great thing in this world is, not so much where we stand, as in what direction we are moving.
GOETHE

Thank God every morning when you get up that you have something to do which must be done, whether you like it or not. Being forced to work, and forced to do your best, will breed in you temperance, self-control, diligence, strength of will, content, and a hundred other virtues which the idle never know.
CHARLES KINGSLEY

Unless we perform divine service with every willing act of our life, we never perform it at all.
JOHN RUSKIN

I do not believe in a fate that falls on men however they act; but I do believe in a fate that falls on them unless they act.
G. K. CHESTERTON

One thing, and only one, in this world has eternity stamped upon it. Feelings pass; resolves and thoughts pass; opinions change. What you have done lasts—lasts in you. Through ages, through eternity, what you have done for Christ, that, and only that, you are.
F. W. ROBERTSON

It is not what he has, nor even what he does, which directly expresses the worth of a man, but what he is.
HENRI FRÉDÉRIC AMIEL

Like the star,
    That shines afar,
    Without haste
    And without rest,
Let each man wheel with steady sway
Round the task that rules the day,
    And do his best.

GOETHE

Let us, then, be up and doing,
With a heart for any fate;
Still achieving, still pursuing,
Learn to labor and to wait.

HENRY WADSWORTH LONGFELLOW

When love and skill work
together, expect a masterpiece.

JOHN RUSKIN

The world is blessed
most by those who
do things, and not
by those who merely
talk about them.

JAMES OLIVER

We live in deeds, not years; in thoughts,
not breaths; in feelings, not in figures
on a dial. We should count time by
heart-throbs. He most lives who thinks
most, feels the noblest, acts the best.

PHILIP JAMES BAILEY

All the beautiful sentiments in
the world weigh less than a single
lovely action.

Adversity

Whenever evil befalls us, we ought to ask ourselves, after the suffering, how we can turn it into good. So shall we take occasion, from bitter root, to raise perhaps many flowers.

LEIGH HUNT

Strength is born in the deep silence of long suffering hearts; not amid joy.

FELICIA HEMANS

As in nature, as in art, so in grace; it is rough treatment that gives souls, as well as stones, their lustre. The more the diamond is cut the brighter it sparkles; and in what seems hard dealing, there God has no end in view but to perfect His people.

GUTHRIE

Great minds have purposes, others have wishes. Little minds are tamed and subdued by misfortune; but great minds rise above them.

WASHINGTON IRVING

Just as there comes a warm sunbeam into every cottage window, so comes a love-beam of God's care and pity for every separate need.

NATHANIEL HAWTHORNE

Life is a long lesson in humility.

SIR JAMES M. BARRIE

No affliction would trouble a child of God, if he knew God's reasons for sending it.

G. CAMPBELL MORGAN

It requires greater virtues to support good fortune than bad.

LA ROCHEFOUCAULD

As the tree is fertilized by its own broken branches and fallen leaves, and grows out of its own decay, so men and nations are bettered and improved by trial, and refined out of broken hopes and blighted expectations.

F. W. ROBERTSON

The tests of life are to make, not break us. Trouble may demolish a man's business but build up his character. The blow at the outward man may be the greatest blessing to the inner man. If God, then, puts or permits anything hard in our lives, be sure that the real peril, the real trouble, is that we shall lose if we flinch or rebel.

M. D. BABCOCK

He who has not tasted bitter does not know what sweet is.

FROM THE GERMAN

We never have more than we can bear. The present hour we are always able to endure. As our day, so is our strength. If the trials of many years were gathered into one, they would overwhelm us; therefore, in pity to our little strength, He sends first one, and then another, then removes both, and lays on a third, heavier perhaps than either; but all is so wisely measured to our strength that the bruised reed is never broken. We do not enough look at our trials in this continuous and successive view. Each one is sent to teach us something, and altogether they have a lesson which is beyond the power of any to teach alone.

H. E. MANNING

The world has been forced to its knees. Unhappily we seldom find our way there without being beaten to it by suffering.

ANNE MORROW LINDBERGH

There are few positions in life in which difficulties have not to be encountered. These difficulties are, however, our best instructors as our mistakes often form our best experience. We learn wisdom from failure more than from success. We often discover what will do by finding out what will not do. Horne Tooke used to say that he had become all the better acquainted with the country from having had the good luck sometimes to lose his way. Great thoughts, discoveries, inventions have very generally been nurtured in hardship, often pondered over in sorrow and established with difficulty.

⁓Paxton Hood

Go, bury thy sorrow,
    The world hath its share;
Go, bury it deeply,
    Go, hide it with care.
Go, bury thy sorrow,
    Let others be blest;
Go, give them the sunshine,
    And tell God the rest.

Be not afraid in misfortune. When God causes a tree to be hewn down He takes care that His birds can nestle on another.

⁓Anonymous

God sometimes shuts the door
    and shuts us in,
That He may speak, perchance
    through grief or pain,
And softly, heart to heart, above the din,
May tell some precious thought
    to us again.

⁓Anonymous

The beautiful is as useful as the useful, perhaps more so.

— VICTOR HUGO

The human heart yearns for the beautiful in all ranks of life.

— HARRIET BEECHER STOWE

Zest is the secret of all beauty. There is no beauty that is attractive without zest.

— CHRISTIAN DIOR

Those who dwell among the beauties and mysteries of the earth are never alone or weary of life.

— RACHEL CARSON

Some people, no matter how old they get, never lose their beauty—they merely move it from their faces into their hearts.

— ANONYMOUS

Far away there in the sunshine are my highest aspirations. I may not reach them, but I can look up and see their beauty, believe in them, and try to follow where they lead.

— LOUISA MAY ALCOTT

I don't think all of the misery, but all of the beauty that still remains.

— ANNE FRANK

Did it ever strike you that goodness is not merely a beautiful thing, but by far the most beautiful thing in the whole world? So that nothing is to be compared for value with goodness; that riches, honor, power, pleasure, learning, the whole world and all in it, are not worth having in comparison with being good; and the utterly best thing for a man is to be good, even though he were never to be rewarded for it.

— Charles Kingsley

Beauty is but the sensible image of the Infinite.— Like truth and justice it lives within us; like virtue and the moral law it is a companion of the soul.

— Bancroft

Every year of my life I grow more convinced that it is wisest and best to fix our attention on the beautiful and the good, and dwell as little as possible on the evil and the false.

— Cecil

After all, it is the divinity within that makes the divinity without; and I have been more fascinated by a woman of talent and intelligence, though deficient in personal charms, than I have been by the most regular beauty.

— Washington Irving

That which is striking and beautiful is not always good; but that which is good is always beautiful.

— Ninon de l'Enclos

There is no beautifier of complexion, or form, or behavior, like the wish to scatter joy and not pain around us.

RALPH WALDO EMERSON

Beauty does not lie in the face. It lies in the harmony between man and his industry. Beauty is expression. When I paint a mother I try to render her beautiful by the mere look she gives her child.

JEAN FRANÇOIS MILLET

The beauty seen is partly in him who sees it.

BOVEE

If God took time to create beauty, how can we be too busy to appreciate it?

RANDALL B. CORBIN

Cheerfulness and content are great beautifiers and are famous preservers of youthful looks.

CHARLES DICKENS

Goodness and love mould the form into their own image, and cause the joy and beauty of love to shine forth from every part of the face. When this form of love is seen, it appears ineffably beautiful, and affects with delight the inmost life of the soul.

EMANUEL SWEDENBORG

Courage

Courage consists not in hazarding without fear, but being resolutely minded in just cause. The brave man is not he who feels no fear, for that were stupid and irrational, but he whose noble soul subdues its fear, and bravely dares the danger nature shrinks from.

FERROLD

No man is worth his salt who is not ready at all times to risk his body, to risk his well-being, to risk his life, in a great cause.

THEODORE ROOSEVELT

The worst sorrows in life are not in its losses and misfortunes, but its fears.

A. C. BENSON

Courage is resistance to fear, mastery of fear—not absence of fear.

MARK TWAIN

Fear is lack of faith. Lack of faith is ignorance.

HORACE TRAUBEL

Though no friend, no man, be with thee, fear nothing! Thy God is here.

J. E. DINGER

There are always reasons for giving up. Arguments for self-pity are thick as blackberries. The world is crowded with thorns and cruelties, causes for tears. Courage is the divine unreason against which, as against a rock, the waves of disaster beat in vain. Say to yourself: I am unconquerable. I shall arrive. In the center of creation sits not an enemy, but my Friend. I shall arrive—what time, what circuit first, I ask not. In some time, His good time, I shall arrive. Let come what will, I shall never say I am beaten. I am not a negligible molecule, a mote in the sunbeam, a worm! I am a man, and, so help me God! I shall play the man. Failure! There is no such word in all the bright lexicon of speech, unless you yourself have written it there! There is no such thing as failure except to those who accept and believe in failure.

O. S. MARDEN

Courage does not consist in feeling no fear, but in conquering fear. He is the hero who seeing the lions on either side goes straight on, because there his duty lies.

SATURDAY MAGAZINE

I hate to see things done by halves.
If it be right, do it boldly,
if it be wrong, leave it undone.

GILPIN

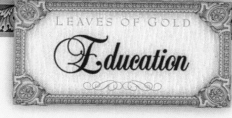

Education

A man should never be ashamed to own he has been in the wrong, which is but saying, in other words, that he is wiser today than he was yesterday.

—Alexander Pope

Educate men without religion, and you make of them but clever devils.

—Duke of Wellington

If you have knowledge, let others light their candles at it.

Everyone is ignorant only on different subjects.

—Will Rogers

Do not mistake acquirement of mere knowledge for power. Like food, these things must be digested and assimilated to become life or force. Learning is not wisdom; knowledge is not necessarily vital energy. The student who has to cram through a school or a college course, who has made himself merely a receptacle for the teacher's thoughts and ideas, is not educated; he has not gained much. He is a reservoir, not a fountain. One retains, the other gives forth. Unless his knowledge is converted into wisdom, into faculty, it will become stagnant like still water.

—J. E. Dinger

Education does not mean teaching people what they do not know. It means teaching them to behave as they do not behave. It is not teaching the youth the shapes of letters and the tricks of numbers, and then leaving them to turn their arithmetic to roguery, and their literature to lust. It means, on the contrary, training them into the perfect exercise and kingly continence of their bodies and souls. It is a painful, continual and difficult work to be done by kindness, by watching, by warning, by precept, and by praise, but above all— by example.

JOHN RUSKIN

I am convinced that we must train not only the head, but the heart and hand as well.

MADAME CHIANG KAI-SHEK

Never mistake knowledge for wisdom. One helps you make a living; the other helps you make a life.

SANDRA CAREY

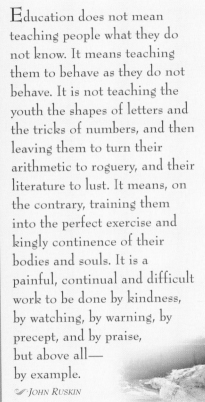

Faith

I will listen to any one's convictions, but pray keep your doubts to yourself.

— GOETHE

I find the doing of the will of God leaves me no time for disputing about His plans.

— GEORGE MACDONALD

Little faith will bring your soul to heaven; great faith will bring heaven to your soul.

— CHARLES H. SPURGEON

It is impossible for that person to despair who remembers that his Helper is omnipotent.

— JEREMY TAYLOR

In every seed to breathe
   the flower,
In every drop of dew
To reverence a cloistered star
Within the distant blue;
To wait the promise of the bow
Despite the cloud between,
Is Faith—the fervid evidence
Of loveliness unseen.

— JOHN B. TABB

It fortifies my soul to know
That though I perish, truth is so;
That, howso'er I stray and range,
Whate'er I do, Thou dost not change.
I steadier step when I recall
That, if I slip, Thou dost not fall.

— ARTHUR HUGH CLOUGH

Faith and obedience are bound up in the same bundle. He that obeys God trusts God; and he that trusts God obeys God.

  CHARLES HADDON SPURGEON

God has a purpose for my life. No other person can take my place. It isn't a big place, to be sure, but for years I have been molded in a peculiar way to fill a peculiar niche in the world's work.

  CHARLES STELZLE

A string of opinions no more constitutes faith, than a string of beads constitutes holiness.

  JOHN WESLEY

I do not want merely to possess a faith; I want a faith that possesses me.

  CHARLES KINGSLEY

All great ages have been ages of belief. I mean, when there was any extraordinary power of performance, when great national movements began, when arts appeared, when heroes existed, when poems were made, the human soul was in earnest.

  RALPH WALDO EMERSON

Such as do not grow in grace, decay in grace. There is no standing at a stay in religion, either we go forward or backward; if faith does not grow, unbelief will; if heavenly mindedness doth not grow, covetousness will.

  T. WATSON

Faith is the subtle chain which binds us to the infinite.

  ELIZABETH OAKES SMITH

I need not shout my faith.
   Thrice eloquent
   Are quiet trees and the green
   listening sod;
Hushed are the stars, whose power
   is never spent;
The hills are mute: yet how
   they speak of God!
CHARLES HANSON TOWNE

There is no unbelief;
Whoever plants a seed beneath
   the sod
And waits to see it push away
   the clod—
He trusts in God.
ELIZABETH YORK CASE

Understanding is the reward of
faith. Therefore seek not to
understand that you may believe, but
believe that you may understand.
AUGUSTINE.

We do not have to go to the
universe to prove the existence of
God from design. We do not have
to dig down into the bowels of the
earth, nor go up to the stars for
proofs of the divine existence. He
is not far from every one of us.
As Paul says, "In Him we move
and have our being"; and as
Tennyson says, "Closer is He than
breathing; and nearer than hands
and feet." God is here. There is
no escaping Him.
PARKHURST

Friendship

Few delights can equal the mere presence of one whom we trust utterly.

— *GEORGE MACDONALD*

We do not wish for friends to feed and clothe our bodies—neighbors are kind enough for that—but to do the like office for our spirits.

— *HENRY DAVID THOREAU*

So long as we love, we serve. So long as we are loved by others I would almost say we are indispensable; and no man is useless while he has a friend.

— *ROBERT LOUIS STEVENSON*

A blessed thing it is for any man or woman to have a friend; one human soul whom we can trust utterly; who knows the best and the worst of us, and who loves us in spite of all our faults; who will speak the honest truth to us, while the world flatters us to our face, and laughs at us behind our back; who will give us counsel and reproof in the day of prosperity and self-conceit; but who, again, will comfort and encourage us in the day of difficulty and sorrow, when the world leaves us alone to fight our own battle as we can.

— *CHARLES KINGSLEY*

If a friend of mine gave a feast, and did not invite me to it, I should not mind a bit. But if a friend of mine had a sorrow and refused to allow me to share it, I should feel it most bitterly. If he shut the doors of the house of mourning against me, I would move back again and again and beg to be admitted, so that I might share in what I was entitled to share.

Oscar Wilde

Blessed are they who have the gift of making friends, for it is one of God's best gifts. It involves many things, but above all, the power of going out of one's self, and appreciating whatever is noble and loving in another.

Thomas Hughes

A friend is one in whom we can confide. The secret chambers of our soul open to his touch on the latch.

J. E. Dinger

Elizabeth Barrett Browning, the poet, asked Charles Kingsley, the novelist, "What is the secret of your life? Tell me, that I may make mine beautiful also." Thinking a moment, the beloved old author replied, "I had a friend."

A friend is one who incessantly pays us the compliment of expecting from us all the virtues, and who can appreciate them in us.

Henry David Thoreau

A friend hears the song in my heart and sings it to me when my memory fails.

Anonymous

The friend who holds up before me the mirror, conceals not my smallest faults, warns me kindly, reproves me affectionately, when I have not performed my duty, he is my friend, however little he may appear so. Again, if a man flattering praises and lauds me, never reproves me, overlooks my faults, and forgives them before I have repented, he is my enemy, however much he may appear my friend.

HERDER

The language of friendship is not words, but meanings. It is an intelligence above language.

ANONYMOUS

Anyone with a heart full of friendship has a hard time finding enemies.

ANONYMOUS

Friendship, in its truest sense, is next to love the most abused of words. One may call many "friend" and be still ignorant of that sentiment, cooler than passion, warmer than respect, more just and generous than either, which recognizes a kindred spirit in another, and, claiming its right, keeps it sacred by the wise reserve that is to friendship what the purple bloom is to the grape, a charm which once destroyed can never be restored.

J. ALCOTT

What a pity that so many people are living with so few friends when the world is full of lonesome strangers who would give anything just to be somebody's friend.

MILO L. ARNOLD

Gratitude

It is a sad thing to reflect that in a world so overflowing with goodness of smell, of fine sights and sweet sounds, we pass by hastily and take so little note of them.

— DAVID GRAYSON

Thou hast given so much to me,
Give one thing more—
   a grateful heart:
Not thankful when it pleaseth
   me,
As if thy blessings had spare days,
But such a heart whose pulse
   may be
Thy praise.

— GEORGE HERBERT

When it comes to life, the critical thing is whether you take things for granted or take them with gratitude.

— G. K. CHESTERTON

Gratitude is born in hearts that take time to count up past mercies.

— CHARLES EDWARD JEFFERSON

So much has been given to me, I have no time to ponder over that which has been denied.

— HELEN KELLER

Cultivate the thankful spirit! It will be to you a perpetual feast.

— JOHN R. MACDUFF

Gratitude is the hardest of all emotions to express. There is no word capable of conveying all that one feels. Until we reach a world where thoughts can be adequately expressed in words, "thank you" will have to do.

A. P. GOUTHEY

It is only with gratitude that life becomes rich.

DIETRICH BONHOEFFER

Pride slays thanksgiving, but a humble mind is the soil out of which thanks naturally grows. A proud man is seldom a grateful man; he never thinks he gets as much as he deserves.

HENRY WARD BEECHER

LEAVES OF GOLD

Happiness

If you ever find happiness by hunting for it, you will find it as the old woman did her lost spectacles, safe on her own nose all the time.

—JOSH BILLINGS

If you want to be miserable think about yourself, about what you want, what you like, what respect people ought to pay you and what people think of you.

—CHARLES KINGSLEY

Those who bring sunshine to the lives of others cannot keep it from themselves.

—JAMES M. BARRIE

It is not the level of prosperity that makes for happiness but the kinship of heart to heart and the way we look at the world. Both attitudes are within our power, so that a man is happy so long as he chooses to be happy, and no one can stop him.

—ALEXANDER SOLZHENITSYN

Happiness is a thing to be practiced, like the violin.

—JOHN LUBBOCK

The happiest people don't necessarily have the best of everything. They just make the best of everything.

We act as though comfort and luxury were the chief requirements of life, when all we need to make us really happy is something to be enthusiastic about.

CHARLES KINGSLEY

What right have I to make every one in the house miserable because I am miserable? Troubles must come to all, but troubles need not be wicked, and it is wicked to be a destroyer of happiness.

AMELIA E. BARR

The moments of happiness we enjoy take us by surprise. It is not that we seize them, but that they seize us.

ASHLEY MONTAGU

Happiness is as a butterfly, which, when pursued, is always just beyond our grasp, but which, if you will sit down quietly, may alight upon you.

NATHANIEL HAWTHORNE

The most unhappy of all men is the man who cannot tell what he is going to do, that has got no work cut out for him in the world, and does not go into any. For work is the grand cure of all the maladies and miseries that ever beset mankind—honest work which you intend getting done.

CARLYLE

You have not fulfilled every duty, unless you have fulfilled that of being pleasant.

CHARLES BUXTON

Heartstrings

There is nothing that makes men rich and strong but that which they carry inside of them. Wealth is of the heart, not of the hand.

~ JOHN MILTON

Hearts that are open to the love that is God, feel loved in loving and served in serving.

~ EDWARD GLOEGGLER

Two things are bad for the heart—running up stairs and running down people.

~ BERNARD BARUCH

Holding a beggar's child
Against my heart,
Through blinding tears I see
That as I love the tiny,
    piteous thing,
So God loves me!

~ TOYOHIKO KAGAWA

The heart that is to be filled to the brim with holy joy must be held still.

~ GEORGE SEATON BOWES

Winter is on my head, but eternal spring is in my heart.

~ VICTOR HUGO

Purge out of every heart the lurking grudge. Give us the grace and strength to forebear and to persevere. Offenders, give us the grace to accept and to forgive offenders. Forgetful ourselves, help us to bear cheerfully the forgetfulness of others. Give us courage and gaiety and the quiet mind. Spare to us our friends, soften to us our enemies.

ROBERT LOUIS STEVENSON

The great man is he who does not lose his child's heart.

MENG-TZU

Have a heart that never hardens, and a temper that never tires, and a touch that never hurts.

CHARLES DICKENS

The only thing that makes one place more attractive to me than another is the quantity of heart I find in it.

JANE WELSH CARLYLE

The holiest of all holidays are those kept by ourselves in silence and apart: the secret anniversaries of the heart.

HENRY WADSWORTH LONGFELLOW

What the heart has once owned and had, it shall never lose.

HENRY WARD BEECHER

LEAVES OF GOLD

Home & Family

Every house where love abides and friendship is a guest, is surely home, and home, sweet home, for there the heart can rest.

HENRY VAN DYKE

He is the happiest, be he king or peasant, who finds peace in his home.

GOETHE

The bravest battle that ever was fought!
Shall I tell you where and when?
On the maps of the world you will find it not;
'Twas fought by the mothers of men.

JOAQUIN MILLER

Most of us become parents long before we have stopped being children.

M. McLAUGHLIN

Sweet is the smile of home;
the mutual look,
When hearts are of each other sure.

JOHN KEBLE

Most of all the other beautiful things in life come by twos and threes, by dozens and hundreds. Plenty of roses, stars, sunsets, rainbows, brothers and sisters, aunts and cousins, but only one mother in the whole world.

KATE DOUGLAS WIGGIN

Home is a place where the great are small, and the small are great.

ANONYMOUS

Better the cottage where one is merry than the palace where one weeps.

CHINESE PROVERB

Whoe'er thou art that entereth
   here,
Forget the struggling world
And every trembling fear.
Here all belong to God above.
Thou, too, dear heart: and here
   the rule of life is love.

ANONYMOUS

Happiness grows at our own
firesides, and is not to be
picked in strangers' gardens.

DOUGLAS JERROLD

Our home joys are the most
delightful earth affords, and the
joy of parents in their children is
the most holy joy of humanity. It
makes their hearts pure and
good; it lifts men up to their
Father in heaven.

JOHANN HEINRICH PESTALOZZI

Family faces are magic mirrors.
Looking at people who belong to
us, we see the past, present and
future.

GAIL LUMET BUCKLEY

A house without love may be
a castle, or a palace, but it is not
a home; love is the life of a true
home. A home without love is
no more a home than a body
without a soul is a man.

JOHN LUBBOCK

Home, a place that our feet
may leave, but not our hearts.

ANONYMOUS

We never know the love of
a parent till we become
parents ourselves.

HENRY WARD BEECHER

40

There is never much trouble in any family where the children hope someday to resemble their parents.

— WILLIAM LYON PHELPS

What is home?
A world of strife shut out—
a world of love shut in.
The only spot on earth where
faults and failings of fallen
humanity are hidden under
the mantle of charity.
The father's kingdom,
the children's paradise,
the mother's world.
Where you are treated the best
and grumble the most.

— ANONYMOUS

Govern a small family as you would cook a small fish— very gently.

— CHINESE PROVERB

Immortality

It is not darkness you are going to, for God is Light. It is not lonely, for Christ is with you. It is not an unknown country, for Christ is there.

☙ CHARLES KINGSLEY

Out of the pain of night-watching
　　removed
Into the sleep that God gives His
　　beloved,
Into the dawn of a glad resurrection,
Into the house of unbroken affection,
Into the joy of her Lord—
　　thence confessing
Death in disguise is His angel
　　in blessing.

☙ ANONYMOUS

There is only one way to get ready for immortality, and that is to love this life and live it as bravely and faithfully, and cheerfully as we can.

☙ HENRY VAN DYKE

How shall I express my thought of it? It is not mere existence, however prolonged and free from annoyance. It is not the pleasures of the senses, however vivid. It is not peace. It is not happiness. It is not joy. But it is all these combined into one condition of spiritual perfection—one emotion of indescribable rapture—the peace after the storm has gone by, the soft repose after the grief is over, the joy of victory when the conflict is ended.

☙ HILL

I know the night is near at hand:
The mists lie low on hill and bay,
The Autumn sheaves are dewless, dry;
But I have had the day.
Yes, I have had, dear Lord, the day;
When at Thy call I have the night,
Brief be the twilight as I pass
From light to dark, from dark
　　to light.

☙ SILAS WEIR MITCHELL

Our hope for eternal life in the hereafter does not spring from a longing for a spiritual existence, but grows out of our love for life upon this earth, which we have tried and found good.

ROBERT J. SHORES

Everything science has taught me—and continues to teach me strengthens my belief in the continuity of our spiritual existence after death.

WERNHER VON BRAUN

Join thyself to the eternal God, and thou shalt be eternal.

AUGUSTINE

Death to a good man is but passing through a dark entry, out of one little dusky room of his Father's house into another that is fair and large, lightsome and glorious, and divinely entertaining.

A. CLARKE

Seems it strange that thou shouldst live forever? Is it less strange that thou shouldst live at all?

EDWARD YOUNG

Millions long for immortality who do not know what to do with themselves on a rainy Sunday afternoon.

SUSAN ERTZ

LEAVES OF GOLD

Joy

Real joy comes not from riches or from the praise of men, but from doing something worthwhile.

Joy is not in things, it is in us.
— RICHARD WAGNER

True joy is not a thing of moods, not a capricious emotion, tied to fluctuating experiences. It is a state and condition of the soul. It survives through pain and sorrow and, like a subterranean spring, waters the whole life. It is intimately allied and bound up with love and goodness, and so is deeply rooted in the life of God.
— RUFUS MATTHEW JONES

There can be no real and abiding happiness without sacrifice. Our greatest joys do not result from our efforts toward self-gratification, but from a loving and spontaneous service to other lives. Joy comes not to him who seeks it for himself, but to him who seeks it for other people.
— H. W. SYLVESTER

We miss the really great joys of life scrambling for bargain-counter happiness.
— ROY L. SMITH

It is a poor heart that never rejoices.
— ANONYMOUS

I have met people so empty of joy that when I clasped their frosty fingertips it seemed as if I were shaking hands with a northeast storm. Others there are whose hands have sunbeams in them, so that their grasp warms my heart. It may be only the clinging touch of a child's hand, but there is as much potential sunshine in it for me as there is in a loving glance for others.

HELEN KELLER

Let your mind be playful and you will enjoy life better.

ANONYMOUS

One joy dispels a hundred cares.

CHINESE PROVERB

People need joy, quite as much as clothing. Some of them need it far more.

MARGARET COLLIER GRAHAM

Joy is never in our power, and pleasure is. I doubt whether anyone who has tasted joy would ever, if both were in his power, exchange it for all the pleasure in the world.

C. S. LEWIS

Joy can be real only if people look upon their life as a service, and have a definite object in life outside themselves and their personal happiness.

LEO TOLSTOY

Take joy home,
And make a place in thy great heart for her,
And give her time to grow, and cherish her!
Then will she come and often sing to thee
When thou art working in the furrows; ay,
Or weeding in the sacred hour of dawn.
It is a comely fashion to be glad.
Joy is the grace we say to God.

JEAN INGELOW

There is no such thing as the pursuit of
happiness, but there is the discovery of joy.

JOYCE GRENFELL

The reflection on a day well spent
furnishes us with joys more pleasing
than ten thousand truimphs.

THOMAS À KEMPIS

Kindness

Though the world needs reproof and correction, it needs kindness more; though it needs the grasp of the strong hand, it needs, too, the open palm of love and tenderness.

HENRY WARD BEECHER

The person who sows seeds of kindness will have a perpetual harvest.

ANONYMOUS

If I can put one touch of rosy sunset into the life of any man or woman, I shall feel that I have worked with God.

GEORGE MACDONALD

Life is short and we have not too much time for gladdening the hearts of those who are traveling the dark way with us. Oh, be swift to love! Make haste to be kind!

HENRI FRÉDÉRIC AMIEL

The best portions of a good
    man's life—
His little, nameless,
    unremembered acts
Of kindness and love.

WILLIAM WORDSWORTH

There is a grace of kind listening, as well as a grace of kind speaking.

FREDERICK WILLIAM FABER

In a remote district of Wales a baby boy lay dangerously ill. The widowed mother walked five miles through the night in the drenching rain to get the doctor. He hesitated about making the unpleasant trip. He questioned, "Would it pay?" He knew that he would receive little money for his services, and besides, if the child were saved, he would only become a poor laborer. But love for humanity and a sense of professional responsibility conquered, and the little child's life was saved. Years after when this same child became first Chancellor of the Exchequer, and later Prime Minister of England, the old doctor said, "I never dreamed that in saving that child on the farm hearth, I was saving the life of a national leader." God is constantly justified in the responsibilities He has placed upon us for showing kindness to one another.

Ask Him to increase your powers of sympathy: to give you more quickness and depth of sympathy, in little things as well as great. Opportunities of doing a kindness are often lost from mere want of thought. Half a dozen lines of kindness may bring sunshine into the whole day of some sick person. Think of the pleasure you might give to some one who is much shut up, and who has fewer pleasures than you have, by sharing with her some little comfort or enjoyment that you have learned to look upon as a necessary of life.

G. H. WILKINSON

Kindness is loving people more than they deserve.

JOSEPH JOUBERT

Kind words toward those
    you daily meet,
Kind words and actions right,
Will make this life of ours
    most sweet,
Turn darkness into night.

ISAAC WATTS

Kind words are the music of the world. They have a power which seems to be beyond natural causes, as though they were some angel's song which had lost its way and come to earth.

FREDERICK WILLIAM FABER

Life Lessons

We can read poetry, and recite poetry, but to live poetry—is the symphony of life.

S. FRANCES FOOTE

It is great—and there is no other greatness—to make one nook of God's creation more fruitful, better, more worthy of God; to make some human heart a little wiser, manlier, happier, more blessed, less accursed.

THOMAS CARLYLE

The dedicated life is the life worth living. You must give with your whole heart.

ANNIE DILLARD

Three men, all engaged at the same employment, were asked what they were doing. One said he was making five dollars a day. Another replied that he was cutting stone. The third said he was building a cathedral. The difference was not in what they were actually doing, although the spirit of the third might quite possibly have made him the more expert at his task. They were all earning the same wage; they were all cutting stone; but only one held it in his mind that he was helping build a great edifice. Life meant more to him than to his mates, because he saw further and more clearly.

ANONYMOUS

I avoid looking forward or backward, and try to keep looking upward.

Charlotte Brontë

Every soul that touches yours—
Be it the slightest contact—
Gets therefrom some good;
Some little grace; one kindly
   thought;
One aspiration yet unfelt;
One bit of courage
For the darkening sky;
One gleam of faith
To brave the thickening ills
   of life;
One glimpse of brighter skies—
To make this life worthwhile
And heaven a surer heritage.

George Eliot

As a cure for worrying, work is better than whiskey.

Thomas A. Edison

We cannot tell what may happen to us in the strange medley of life. But we can decide what happens in us—how we can take it, what we do with it—and that is what really counts in the end. How to take the raw stuff of life and make it a thing of worth and beauty—that is the test of living. Life is an adventure of faith, if we are to be victors over it, not victims of it.

Anonymous

Fear not that thy life shall come to an end, but rather fear that it shall never have a beginning.

J. H. Newman

He is a wise man who does not grieve for the things which he has not, but rejoices for those which he has.

Epictetus

There's only one corner of the universe you can be certain of improving, and that's your own self. So you have to begin there, not outside, not on other people. That comes afterwards, when you have worked on your own corner.

ALDOUS HUXLEY

Live for something. Do good and leave behind you a monument of virtue that the storm of time can never destroy. Write your name in kindness, love, and mercy on the hearts of thousands you come in contact with year by year; you will never be forgotten. No, your name, your deeds will be as legible on the hearts you leave behind as the stars on the brow of evening. Good deeds will shine as the stars of heaven.

CHALMERS

I asked God for all things so I could enjoy life. He gave me life so I could enjoy all things.

ANONYMOUS

God, make my life a little
    flower
That giveth joy to all;
Content to bloom in native
    bower
Although its place be small.

MATILDA B. EDWARD

My business is not to remake myself, but to make the absolute best of what God made.

ROBERT BROWNING

Life was meant to be lived, and curiosity must be kept alive. One must never, for whatever reason, turn his back on life.

ELEANOR ROOSEVELT

Life is no brief candle to me. It is a sort of splendid torch which I have got hold of for the moment, and I want to make it burn as brightly as possible before handing it on to future generations.

🖋 *George Bernard Shaw*

I accept life unconditionally. Life holds so much—so much to be so happy about always. Most people ask for happiness on condition. Happiness can be felt only if you don't set conditions.

🖋 *Arthur Rubenstein*

We are born helpless. As soon as we are fully conscious we discover loneliness. We need others physically, emotionally, intellectually. We need them if we are to know anything, even ourselves.

🖋 *C. S. Lewis*

Everything in life that we really accept undergoes a change. So suffering must become love. That is the mystery.

🖋 *Katherine Mansfield*

You will find, as you look back upon your life, that the moments when you have really lived are the moments when you have done things in the spirit of love.

🖋 *Henry Drummond*

Your life is a coin. You can spend it any way you wish, but you can spend it only once.

🖋 *Lillian Dickson*

There is not enough darkness in all the world to put out the light of one small candle.

🖋 *Anonymous*

LEAVES OF GOLD

Love

*D*o right, and God's recompense to you will be the power of doing more right. Give, and God's reward to you will be the spirit of giving more; a blessed spirit, for it is the Spirit of God Himself, whose Life is the blessedness of giving. Love, and God will pay you with the capacity of more love; for love is Heaven— love is God within you.

~ F. W. ROBERTSON

There is a wealth of un-expressed love in the world.

~ ARTHUR HOPKINS

No burden is too heavy when it is carried with love.

~ ANONYMOUS

Where there is great love there are always miracles.

~ WILLA CATHER

Love may strive, but vain is the endeavor
All its boundless riches to unfold;
Still its tenderest, truest secrets linger
Ever in the deepest depth untold.

~ ADELAIDE A. PROCTER

Every year I live I am more
convinced that the waste of
life lies in the love we have not
given, the powers we have not
used, the selfish prudence
that will risk nothing, and
which, shirking pain, misses
happiness as well.

Mary Cholmondeley

How sweet the words of truth
breathed from the lips of love.

James Beattie

Life has taught us that love
does not consist in gazing at
each other but in looking
outward together in the
same direction.

Antoine de Saint-Exupéry

To love some one more
    dearly every day,
To help a wandering child
    to find his way,
To ponder o'er a noble
    thought and pray,
And smile when evening
    falls—
        This is my task.

Maude Louise Ray

Everyone has experienced
that truth: that love, like a
running brook, is disregarded,
taken for granted; but when
the brook freezes over, then
people begin to remember how
it was when it ran, and they
want it to run again.

Kahlil Gibran

For one human being to love another; that is perhaps the most difficult of all our tasks, the ultimate, the last test and proof, the work for which all other work is but preparation.

RAINER MARIA RILKE

Love is an act of endless forgiveness, a tender look which becomes a habit.

PETER USTINOV

Where love is concerned, too much is not even enough!

DE BEAUMARCHAIS

The great tragedy of life is not that men perish, but that they cease to love.

W. SOMERSET MAUGHAM

If you have love in your heart, you will always have something to give.

ANONYMOUS

Love is but the discovery of ourselves in others, and the delight in the recognition.

ALEXANDER SMITH

What is Love? I have met in the streets a very poor young man who was in love. His hat was old, his coat worn, the water passed through his shoes and the stars through his soul.

VICTOR HUGO

What is lovely never dies
But passes into other
    loveliness,
Star-dust, or sea foam,
    flower or winged air.

THOMAS BAILEY ALDRICH

Do not keep the alabaster box of your love and friendship sealed up until your friends are dead. Fill their lives with sweetness. Speak approving, cheering words while their ears can hear them, and while their hearts can be thrilled and made happier. The kind things you mean to say when they are gone, say before they go.

GEORGE W. CHILDS

Love is the doorway through which the human soul passes from selfishness to service and from solitude to kinship with all mankind.

ANONYMOUS

LEAVES OF GOLD

Nature's Garden

To own a bit of ground, to scratch it with a hoe, to plant seeds, and watch their renewal of life, this is the commonest delight of the race, the most satisfactory thing a man can do.

CHARLES DUDLEY WARNER

Flowers always make people better, happier, and more helpful; they are sunshine, food and medicine to the soul.

LUTHER BURBANK

He who is born with a silver spoon in his mouth is generally considered a fortunate person, but his good fortune is small compared to that of the happy mortal who enters this world with a passion for flowers in his soul.

CELIA THAXTER

Apprentice yourself to nature. Not a day will pass without her opening a new and wondrous world of experience to learn from and enjoy.

RICHARD W. LANGER

Everybody needs beauty as well as bread, places to play in and pray in, where Nature may heal and cheer and give strength to body and soul alike.

JOHN MUIR

Love of flowers and all things green and growing is with many women a passion so strong that it often seems to be a sort of primal instinct, coming down through generation after generation.

HELENA RUTHERFORD ELY

God spoke! and from the arid scene
Sprang rich and verdant bowers,
Till all the earth was soft with green,—
He smiled; and there were flowers.

MARY MCNEIL FENOLLOSA

Everywhere I find the signature, the autograph of God, and he will never deny his own handwriting. God hath set his tabernacle in the dewdrop as surely as in the sun. No man can any more create the smallest flower than he could create the greatest world.

JOSEPH PARKER

Perhaps the chiefest attraction of a garden is that occupation can always be found there. With mind and fingers busy, cares are soon forgotten.

ALICIA AMHERST

The lesson I have thoroughly learnt, and wish to pass on to others, is to know the enduring happiness that the love of a garden gives. I rejoice when I see anyone, and especially children, inquiring about flowers, and wanting gardens of their own, and carefully working in them. For love of gardening is a seed that once sown never dies, but always grows and grows to an enduring and ever increasing source of happiness.

GERTRUDE JEKYLL

People from a planet without flowers would think we must be mad with joy the whole time to have such things about us.

IRIS MURDOCH

A modest garden contains, for those who know how
to look and to wait, more instruction than a library.

HENRI FRÉDÉRIC AMIEL

We cannot fathom the mystery of a single flower,
nor is it intended we should....

JOHN RUSKIN

Each moment of the year has
its own beauty...a picture
which was never seen
before and which shall
never be seen again.

RALPH WALDO EMERSON

Where you tend
a rose, my lad,
a thistle cannot grow.

FRANCES HODGSON BURNETT

LEAVES OF GOLD

Possessions

*H*eap on other men the gift
of riches, but give to me
the gift of the untroubled heart.

— *FROM AN ANCIENT POEM*

Not till we have lost the world
do we begin to find ourselves.

— *HENRY DAVID THOREAU*

The greatest humbug in the world
is the idea that money can make
a man happy. I never had any
satisfaction with mine until I
began to do good with it.

— *C. PRATT*

Poverty is no disgrace to a man
but it is confoundedly inconvenient.

— *SYDNEY SMITH*

I am rich today, a baby ran to meet me,
And put her tiny hand within my own
And smiled, her rosy lips a flower,
The light within her eyes,
    from heaven shone.
And when I crossed the fields the
    birds were singing,
A golden blossom in my pathway lay,
It wasn't much; but, oh, the joy there's
    in it,
To have a baby smile at you
        In just that way.

— *MARGUERITE A. GUTSCHOW*

Wealth consists not in having
possessions but in having
few wants.

— *ESTHER DE WAAL*

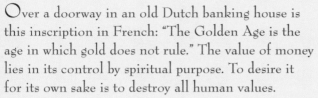

Over a doorway in an old Dutch banking house is this inscription in French: "The Golden Age is the age in which gold does not rule." The value of money lies in its control by spiritual purpose. To desire it for its own sake is to destroy all human values.

Anonymous

It's good to have money and the things that money can buy, but it's good, too, to check up once in a while and make sure you haven't lost the things that money can't buy.

George Horace Lorimer

Everything in the world can be endured, except continual prosperity.

Goethe

Superfluous wealth can buy superfluities only. Money is not required to buy one necessary of the soul.

Henry David Thoreau

LEAVES OF GOLD

Prayer

Thou hast made us for Thyself, O Lord; and our heart is restless until it rests in Thee.

— *AUGUSTINE*

I have lived long enough to thank God that all my prayers have not been answered.

— *JEAN INGELOW*

Any heart turned God-ward, feels more joy in one short hour of prayer, than e'er was raised by all the feasts on earth since its foundation.

— *BAILEY*

God brings no man into the conflicts of life to desert him. Every man has a Friend in Heaven whose resources are unlimited; and on Him he may call at any hour and find sympathy and assistance.

— *MORRIS*

Those who run from God in the morning will scarcely find him the rest of the day.

— *JOHN BUNYAN*

A prayer in its simplest definition is merely a wish turned Godward.

— *PHILLIPS BROOKS*

Lord, what a change within us
    one short hour
Spent in Thy presence will
    avail to make!
What heavy burdens from our
    bosoms take!
What parched grounds refresh
    as with a shower!
We kneel, and all around us
    seem to lower;
We rise, and all, the distant
    and the near,
Stands forth in sunny outline,
    brave and clear;
We kneel, how weak; we rise,
    how full of power!

Why, therefore, should we do
    ourselves this wrong,
Or others—that we are not
    always strong—
That we are sometimes over
    borne with care—
That we should ever weak or
    heartless be,
Anxious or troubled—
    when with us is prayer,
And joy and strength and
    courage are with Thee?

RICHARD C. TRENCH

LEAVES OF GOLD

Serenity

*Quiet minds can not be
perplexed or frightened,
but go on in fortune or misfortune
at their own private pace, like a
clock during a thunderstorm.*

ROBERT LOUIS STEVENSON

I have sought repose everywhere,
and I have found it only in a
little corner with a little book.

ST. FRANCOIS DE SALES

What sweet delight a
quiet life affords.

WILLIAM HAWTHORDEN DRUMMOND

It is when a man is alone,
away from the influence of other
men and their acts, that he can
work on himself. It is in solitude
that he must correct his
thoughts, driving out the bad
and stimulating the good.

LEO TOLSTOY

And so, beside the silent sea,
    I wait the muffled oar;
No harm from Him can come
    to me
On ocean or on shore.

JOHN GREENLEAF WHITTIER

It is in silence that God is
known, and through mysteries
that he declares himself.

ROBERT H. BENSON

Drop thy still dews of quietness,
Till all our strivings cease;
Take from our souls the strain
    and stress,
And let our ordered lives confess
The beauty of thy peace.

JOHN GREENLEAF WHITTIER

Everything true and great grows
in silence. Without silence we
fall short of reality and cannot
plumb the depths of being.

LADISLAUS BOROS

The greatest ideas, the most profound thoughts, and the most beautiful poetry are born from the womb of silence.
WILLIAM ARTHUR WARD

People who cannot bear to be alone are the worst company.
ALBERT GUINON

The ability to speak several languages is an asset, but the ability to keep your mouth shut in one language is priceless.
ANCIENT PROVERB

We have developed a phobia of being alone. We prefer the most trivial and even obnoxious company, the most meaningless activities, to being alone with ourselves; we seem to be frightened at the prospect of facing ourselves.
ERICH FROMM

To know one's self is the true;
To strive with one's self is the good;
To conquer one's self is the beautiful.
JOSEPH ROUX

Practice the art of aloneness and you will discover the treasure of tranquility. Develop the art of solitude and you will unearth the gift of serenity.
WILLIAM ARTHUR WARD

True silence is the rest of the mind and is to the spirit what sleep is to the body, nourishment and refreshment.
WILLIAM PENN

Everything has its wonders, even darness and silence.
HELEN ADAMS KELLER

Silence is but a rich pause in the music of life.
SAROJINI NAIDU

78

Serving Others

The longer I live the more I am convinced that the one thing worth living for and dying for is the privilege of making someone more happy and more useful. No man who ever does anything to lift his fellows ever makes a sacrifice.

BOOKER T. WASHINGTON

There is a loftier ambition than merely to stand high in the world. It is to stoop down and lift those around us a little higher.

HENRY VAN DYKE

There is no happiness in having and getting, but only in giving. Half the world is on the wrong scent in the pursuit of happiness.

F. W. GUNSAULUS

I slept, and I dreamed that life was all joy. I woke, and saw that life was but service. I served, and discovered that service was joy.

RABINDRANATH TAGORE

What do we live for, if it is not to make life less difficult to each other?

GEORGE ELIOT

No one is useless in this world who lightens the burdens of it for another.

CHARLES DICKENS

If you sit down at set of sun
And count the acts that you
    have done,
And, counting, find one
    self-denying deed, one word
That eased the heart of him who
    heard—
One glance most kind,
That fell like sunshine where it
    went—
Then you may count that day
    well spent.

GEORGE ELIOT

When people are serving,
life is no longer meaningless.

JOHN W. GARDNER

We ought to do good to others as simply and as naturally as a horse runs, or a bee makes honey, or a vine bears grapes season after season without thinking of the grapes it has borne.

MARCUS AURELIUS

Even if it's a little thing, do something for those who have need of help, something for which you get no pay but the privilege of doing it.

ALBERT SCHWEITZER

When we serve, we rule;
When we give, we have;
When we surrender ourselves,
    we are victors.

JOHN HENRY NEWMAN

Have you ever had your day suddenly turn sunshiny because of a cheerful word? Have you ever wondered if this could be the same world, because someone had been unexpectedly kind to you? You can make today the same for somebody. It is only a question of a little imagination, a little time and trouble. Think now, "What can I do today to make someone happy?"— old persons, children, servants—even a bone for the dog, or sugar for the bird! Why not?

M. D. Babcock

LEAVES OF GOLD
Spiritual Insights

*N*ever be afraid of giving up your best, and God will give you His better.

   Hinton

*G*od is very patient. It took him years to teach me to say two words: "Lord, anything!"

   A. Douglas Brown

*I*f religion has done nothing for your temper, it has done nothing for your soul.

   Clayton

*L*earn to hold loosely all that is not eternal.

   Agnes Maud Royden

*T*he only lasting treasure is spiritual; the only perfect freedom is serving God.

   Malcolm Muggeridge

*T*alking with humorist Mark Twain, a man commented that his greatest ambition was to visit Mt. Sinai and there see the place where God gave Moses the Ten Commandments. Mark Twain responded by saying, "Why don't you just stay home and keep the Ten Commandments?"

*Y*ou may trust the Lord too little, but you can never trust him too much.

   Anonymous

Dr. Forsyth has told how a friend of his was on a sheep farm in Australia and saw the owner take a little lamb and place it in a huge enclosure where there were several thousand sheep whose bleating, together with the shouting of the sheep-shearers, was deafening. Then the lamb uttered its feeble cry, and the mother sheep at the other end of the enclosure heard it and started to find her lamb. "Do not imagine that you are beyond the reach of the Good Shepherd," said the preacher. "He sees you, He hears you, every good desire of yours is known to Him, and every secret longing for better things. He sees you as if there were no other child in the whole world."

Anonymous

I thank thee, O Lord, that thou hast so set eternity within my heart that no earthly thing can ever satisfy me wholly.

John Baillie

God did not write solo parts for very many of us. He expects us to be participants in the great symphony of life.

Donald Tippett

Our Father refreshes us on the journey with some pleasant inns, but will not encourage us to mistake them for home.

C. S. Lewis

How often we look upon God as our last and feeblest resource! We go to Him because we have no where else to go. And then we learn that the storms of life have driven us, not upon the rocks, but into the desired havens.

GEORGE MACDONALD

Until a man has found God, and been found by God, he begins at no beginning and works to no end.

H. G. WELLS

I leave God's secrets to Himself.— It is happy for me that God makes me of His court, and not of His council.

JOSEPH HALL

No one has a right to look with contempt on himself when God has shown such an interest in him.

ANONYMOUS

Life passes, riches fly away, popularity is fickle, the senses decay, the world changes. One alone is true to us; One alone can be all things to us; One alone can supply our need.

JOHN HENRY NEWMAN

How great a God we need; and how much greater is our God than our greatest need.

ANONYMOUS

LEAVES OF GOLD

Today

*Banish the future;
live only for the hour
and its allotted work. Think
not of the amount to be
accomplished, the difficulties
to be overcome, but set earnestly
at the little task at your elbow,
letting that be sufficient for the
day; for surely our plain duty is
"not to see what lies dimly at a
distance, but to do what lies
clearly at hand."*

OSLER

I expect to pass through this
world but once. Any good thing,
therefore, that I can do or any
kindness I can show to any
fellow human being let me
do it now. Let me not defer
nor neglect it, for I shall not
pass this way again.

STEPHEN GRELLET

Every morning is a fresh
beginning. Every day is
the world made new. Today is
a new day. Today is my world
made new. I have lived all my life
up to this moment, to come to
this day. This moment—this
day—is as good as any moment
in all eternity. I shall make
of this day—a heaven on earth.
This is my day of opportunity.

DAN CUSTER

One of the most tragic things
I know about human nature
is that all of us tend to put off
living. We are all dreaming of
some magical rose garden over
the horizon—instead of enjoying
the roses that are blooming
outside our windows today.

DALE CARNEGIE

Love every day. Each one is so short and they are so few.

NORMAN VINCENT PEALE

Dost thou love life? then do not squander time, for that is the stuff life is made of.

BENJAMIN FRANKLIN

We can better appreciate the miracle of a sunrise if we have waited in darkness.

ANONYMOUS

I still find each day too short for all the thoughts I want to think, all the walks I want to take, all the books I want to read, and all the friends I want to see. The longer I live, the more my mind dwells upon the beauty and wonder of the world.

JOHN BURROUGHS

Light tomorrow with today.

ELIZABETH BARRETT BROWNING

Make a rule, and pray God to help you to keep it, never, if possible, to lie down at night without being able to say, "I have made one human being, at least, a little wiser, a little happier, or a little better this day."

CHARLES KINGSLEY

He who neglects the present moment throws away all he has.

JOHANN FRIEDRICH VON SCHILLER

Time isn't a commodity, something you pass around like cake. Time is the substance of life. When anyone asks you to give your time, they are really asking for a chunk of your life.

ANTOINETTE BOSCO

LEAVES OF GOLD

Worthwhile Thoughts

You never really leave a place you love. Part of it you take with you, leaving a part of you behind.

ANONYMOUS

What to remember,—what to forget,—that is the question. It seems to me that the good things, the heavenly guidance, the help that other men have given us to keep the right path, are the things to remember. The mistakes, the false leads, the devilish influences, are the things to forget.

ANONYMOUS

We can easily forgive a child who is afraid of the dark; the real tragedy of life is when men are afraid of the light.

PLATO

Make no judgments where you have no compassion.

ANNE McCAFFREY

Some lives, like evening primroses, blossom most beautifully in the evening of life.

C. E. COWEN

All truly wise thoughts have been thought already thousands of times; but to make them really ours we must think them over again honestly, till they take firm root in our personal experience.

JOHANN WOLFGANG VON GOETHE

You cannot believe in honor until you have achieved it. Better keep yourself clean and bright: you are the window through which you must see the world.

GEORGE BERNARD SHAW

What sunshine is to flowers, smiles are to humanity. They are but trifles, to be sure but, scattered along life's pathway, the good they do is inconceivable.
Joseph Addison

The capacity to care gives life its deepest significance.
Pablo Casals

If we are truly prudent we shall cherish those noblest and happiest of our tendencies—to love and to confide.
Edward Bulwer-Lytton

It is surely better to pardon too much than to condemn too much.
George Eliot

To understand any living thing you must creep within and feel the beating of its heart.
W. Macneile Dixon

The cure for anything is salt water—sweat, tears, or the sea.
Isak Dinesen

Never get so fascinated by the extraordinary that you forget the ordinary.
Magdalen Nabb

If life were predictable it would cease to be life and be without flavor.
Eleanor Roosevelt

No one grows old by living— only by losing interest in living.
Marie Benton Ray

A single thought in the morning may fill our whole day with joy and sunshine or gloom and depression.
Paramananda

Just as there are no little people or unimportant lives, there is no insignificant work.
Elena Bonner

LEAVES OF GOLD

Illustration Credits

Bridgeman/Art Resource, NY: Pages 42-43, 45.

Fine Art Images, Inc.: Pages 15, 19, 27, 53, 74, 92-93.

Fine Art Photographic Library, Ltd.: Pages Cover, 9, 10,
19, 22, 31, 32, 35, 37, 38, 41, 46, 49, 51, 56, 59, 60,
63, 65, 66, 69, 71, 73, 76, 79, 81, 83, 84, 88, 96.

Giraudon/Art Resource, NY: Pages 75, 91.